Lauer...

from Cousin Edward

Christmas 1928

SOME
DAMAGE
p106

17 April 1979

N.D. but first printing was 1928!

THE
INDISCREET LIMERICK BOOK

THE INDISCREET LIMERICK BOOK

200 NEW EXAMPLES

BY

LANGFORD REED

Author of "The Complete Limerick Book,"
"Sausages and Sundials," "Nonsense
Tales for the Young," etc.

SECOND IMPRESSION

JARROLDS *Publishers* (LONDON)
Limited, 34 Paternoster Row, E.C. 4

Printed in Great Britain by
Woods & Sons, Ltd., London, N. 1

NOTE BY THE AUTHOR

With the exception of a couple of classical allusions, all the place names in this book of Limericks are genuine geographical names, taken either from the Gazetteer of the World, the " A. B. C. Railway Guide," or noted by the author during motoring excursions. He feels rather strongly on this point, for, just as the Geographical Limerick is the Limerick in it's purest and most traditional form, so those examples which are based on imaginary place-names, some of which have been awarded prizes by ignorant adjudicators in newspaper competitions, are outrages upon Limerickal art, and he had to reject more than one well-known example from his " Complete Limerick Book," on this account.

It may, possibly, be of some interest to state that the whole of the specimens in this present collection were perpetrated as a result of that extraordinary morning, a few days before Christmas, 1927, when the ice-sheeted London streets caused many hundreds of casualties. Among other unfortunates, the author fractured his leg and dislocated his ankle and, in consequence, remained a broken Reed for a couple of months. The Abyssinia example, which is the opening "indiscretion" in this book, was composed to amuse his doctor, a few days after the accident and was so well received that the perpetrator was emboldened to spend the greater part of his convalescence in inventing others. Such censure, therefore, as they may provoke, should be laid on the head of the Clerk of the Weather for if that fickle gentleman (or possibly the Clerk is a lady one!) had not misbehaved himself, this volume would certainly not have been compiled!

" Our indiscretion sometimes serves us well."
—*Hamlet*.

" All's not offence that indiscretion finds, and dotage
terms so." —*King Lear*.

Said a doctor in far Abyssinia,
" From the grave I can't possibly win yer ;
   I'm frightfully sorry,
   But the wheel of that lorry
Has made such a big-abyss in yer ! "

There was a young fellow of Acre,
Who took off his hat to a Quaker ;
   When the worthy man said,
   " You are very well bred."
He replied, " Well, you see, I'm a baker ! "

A hairy-kneed native of Alderney,
With hot tea did once badly scald a knee;
   You'll easily see
   Which knee was the knee,
He scalded with tea—it's the balder knee.

Said a good-natured husband of Amhurst,
" Too long I've put up with that Sam
      Hurst :
   Now he, with a fife,
   Serenades my young wife,
And keeps me awake—well then d—
      Hurst ! "

Said an angry old man of Amritsar,
" Have the goodness to mind where you
    spit sir !
  That last shot of yours,
  Has besmirched my plus fours,
You really aren't careful a bit sir ! "

There was an old man of Ankoba,
Who rarely, if ever, was sober ;
  He would drink ev'ry day,
  From the thirteenth of May,
Till the following fifth of October.

A frugal young man from Amoy

A frugal young man, from Amoy,
The waiters shocked, at the Savoy,
   " Some nice bread and dripping,"
   Said he, " would be ripping,
Bring me that and a cold saveloy."

Said a corpulent man, of Argyle,
" I am not really wicked, or vile ;
   The reason I shirk
   My attendance at kirk
Is because I get stuck in the aisle."

A reckless old mot'rist, of Ascot,
His car in a horrid morass got ;
   Said he, to his wife,
    " I don't want to cause strife,
But it's your fault, for losing our mascot ! "

Said a ravenous father of Ashover,
" Is there a plateful of that hash over ? "
   Cried his wife, " Well, there was,
    But there ain't now, because
Young Maudie has spilt it, her sash over ! "

An abnormal P.C., of Asuncion,
Attempted to swallow his truncheon ;
    When they asked, " Are you mad ? "
    He said, " No, but I've had
Too much alcohol with my luncheon ! "

A saucy young flapper of Ayr,
Objected to faces with hair ;
    Said she, " I am chary
    Of lips that are hairy,
My kisses I like to take bare ! "

Said a wife, to her husband, in Bacup,
" I've no wish a scandal to rake-up ;
   But if you have been late
   At the office, then state
Why your coat collar's covered with
     make-up ! "

" I'm peeved ! " cried a sportsman of
     Bagshot,
" For I thought that I had a stag shot,
   I have cause for complaint,
   For I'm blowed if I ain't
Some silly, obtrusive old hag shot ! "

When she went to the Fancy Dress Ball,
In the costume of Eve, at the Fall,
   They remarked that her fig leaves,
   Were little, not big leaves,
So they turned her away from the hall.

There was a young fellow of Bangor,
Possessing remarkable languor ;
   He was saved from the " workus "
   By joining a circus,
As a somnolent clown, under Sanger.

A singular curate of Bantry,
Delighted to rummage the pantry :
   The fruits of his search,
   He took to the church,
And ate at his ease in the chantry.

There was a young man on the beach,
Who cried, " What a peach !　What a
     peach ! "
   When the maid said, with vigour,
   " You libel my figure ; "
He replied, " It's a figure of speech ! "

A cautious young man of Bengal,
Loved a girl exceedingly small :
   Said he, " She's a dove,
   And it's better to love
A short girl than not love a(t all) ! "

A crafty bee-farmer, of Bisbee,
Claimed the bee of a rival as his bee.
   Cried the man, " Not a bit,
   Why I recognise it,
It's my favourite bumble-bee, Thisbe ! "

There was an old man of Black Rock;
Who never wore more than one sock;
  If you say this is quaint,
  I deny it, it ain't!
For he was a one-legged crock.

A stingy old man of the Boyne,
One fell in the sea from a groyne,
  And sent to the coastguard,
  Who saved him, this postcard,
"Your conduct, begorra, was foine!"

Said a destitute chieftain, in Bornu,
To his nose-ring, "For long I have
    wornu :
  But now, from my snout,
  You must vanish.   The drought
Has ruined me quite—I must pornu ! "

There was an old man of Brazil,
Who said, " I have felt very ill,
  Since I dived in the Amazon,
  Without my pyjamas on,
And caught a malarious chill."

Said a humble old person of Brighouse

Said a humble old person of Brighouse,
Who took all his meals in a pig-house,
   " I'd much rather dine
   With these amiable swine
Than feed with the folks in my big
     house ! "

There was an old person of Brussels,
Who feasted on winkles and mussels ;
   Said he, " Mixed with jam,
   And eaten with ham,
They *may* stimulate my corpuscles ! "

There was a young lady of Buckingham,*
Who ate a large goose and two ducking-
    ham ;
  Since having that feast,
  Her girth's so increased,
In her clothing she's let out the tucking-
    ham.

There was a young bounder of Budapest,
Whom you, I feel sure, will concludapest
  He pelted the knees
  Of the flappers with cheese,
Said they, " We have not met a rudapest ! "

* *Bucks.*

There was an old dandy of Calicut,
Who said to his tailor, " This balicut
   I really can't pardon,
   With shears from the garden,
A smarter suit could my girl, Salicut ! "

A critical native of Candia,
Said, " I do not care for the band 'ere ;
   They persistently play
   Nought but Jazz, night and day,
It's music we don't understand 'ere ! "

When they said to a sexton of Canterbury,
" What a long time you take that old
    manterbury ; "
  He replied, in a pet,
  " You seem to forget
I have, also, his step-sister Annterbury ! "

Said a kind-hearted fellow of Canton,
When told he had only one pant on ;
  " My one-legged brother
  Has borrowed the other,
And that's why on my leg it ant on ! "

Said a corpulent man of Catteris,
" My wife than myself much fatter is ;
    My son's fatter yet,
    And I'm open to bet,
My daughter's more fat than the latter is."

A reckless young fellow of Ceuta,
Once rode into church on a scooter ;
    When he knocked down the Dean,
    He said, " Sorry, old bean,
I ought to have sounded my hooter ! "

A modern young lady of Chertsey,
Attempted an old-fashioned curtsey,
   And a couple of carters
   Saw more than her garters,
She had such a very short skirt.   See ?

There was a young lady of Clifton,
Who tried all she could to help thrift on ;
   But provoked many strictures,
   When seen at the pictures,
With only her hat and her shift on !

A sarcastic native of Colon,
The size of his town was most droll on ;
   Said he, " It's so small,
   It is no town at all,
It ought to be called—Semi-Colon ! "

There was a young fellow of Cromer,
Who read, aloud, verses from Homer ;
   Folks came from afar,
   To smell his cigar,
It had such a beautiful odour.

A jolly old sceptic of Crook,
Was visited once by a spook ;
   Said the shameless old sinner,
   " If you'll stay and have dinner,
I'll be pleased to arrange with the cook."

Said the son of the M.P. for Cupar,
" It's my duty to mention to you, Pa,
   You are most indiscreet
   To risk losing your seat
By sitting right down in the glue Pa ! "

Said a cute old codger of Cutch,
" For houses they're asking too much;
   So I'll ask my tame rabbit
   To teach me the habit
Of making my home in a hutch ! "

There was an old man of Dakota,
Exceedingly fond of a bloater;
   Said he, " Let fish-shippers
   Enthuse about kippers,
I don't care for them one iota ! "

Said a vagrant tramping to Darton,
" Do please a lift give me, your cart on."
   Said the carter, " Not me !
   Two's company, not three,
And already I've got my sweetheart on ! "

There was an old lady of Darvel,
Who became a great maritime marvel.
   In her best Sunday robe,
   She sailed twice round the Globe,
With another old girl in a carvel.

There was a small husband of Dawlish,
Whose wife was bad-tempered and
brawlish.
   When they cried to him, " Ted,
   Heave a brick at her head ! "
He answered, " I daren't, she's too
tallish ! "

A lively young damsel, of Deal,
Shocked folks by her deshabille ;
   When they shouted, " Desist ! "
   She replied, " I insist !
My figure is neat and genteel."

There was an old fellow of Detmold,
Who went in the garden and ate mold;
  Said he, " It's quite nice,
  If taken with rice,
But dry mold is nicer than wet mold."

A restless young wifey of Dijon,
Asked, " Why are you staring at me,
    John ? "
  " You're squirming," said he,
  " Have you got a flea ? "
" I'm sorry to say I've got three, John ! "

WHEN A LIMERICK'S LAST WORD DEPENDS

I

Since a Limerick's last word depends
On a rhyme its first couplet portends
Is it chance or design
When the poet's last line
Seems to prove what he firmly contends?

Can one really agree
That the writer is free
To conclude as he blithely intends?

Must it not be assumed
That the author is doomed
To maintaining the line he defends?

Could he hold out the hope
Of exploiting that scope
To which Vanity only pretends?

Is it not a hard fact
That the range must contract
As the length of his poem extends?

Is one then to presume
That the bard will find room
To embellish the text he emends?

Will it not need a Keats
Or that other one—Yeats
To re-straighten the rhymes that he bends?

(1)

Could the confident beat
Of his metrical feat
Stay the course if a blister distends?

Would it not take a Donne
Or the famous Byron
To remodel the rhythms he rends?

Could one faintly suppose
That the last word he "chose"
Is employed for the nuance it lends?

Can one frankly expect
That the bard will "perfect"
Every detail to which he attends?

Will there not come a time
When the lack of a rhyme
Must dictate where his argument tends?

Won't the readership float
Like a rudderless boat
Where the river of Babylon wends?

Will his hand not be forced
Till he ends up divorced
From that plan which he first comprehends?

Could he carry the strain
Of ransacking his brain
To escape from the fate which impends?

Can't the bard understand
That this poem he's planned
Must conflict with statistical trends?

Could one be so naive
As to fondly believe
In the nonsense he hereby appends?

Since a Limerick's last word depends
On a rhyme its first couplet portends
It may seem a poor joke
When the finishing stroke
Is a sentence the poet suspends.

Yet the line that's supressed
Is to shrewdly invest
And eventually yield dividends;

Hence the cause of delay
Is not doubt or dismay
But the policy prudence commends.

But in writing this verse
Would it not be perverse
To just wait till the Muse condescends?

With the words in my hoard
I can better afford
To pay cash for the favours She vends.

For the reader will find
I have made up my mind
To pursue where ambition ascends;

And although this may seem
An impossible dream
It depends on the work one expends.

In concluding a rhyme
On a musical chime
I gave thought to the message it sends:

Listen well with your eye
Silent ears may espy
Secret notes in the tones that it blends.

For the secret of Art
Is to never depart
From that purpose your Will apprehends;

Was the spear that Will shook
And the aim that he took
Not at Countrymen, Romans and Friends?

For this tour de force
I have plotted my course
From the angle its first line subtends;

In a tower de farce
May the bard not surpass
Limitations his talent transcends?

Yet a writer of rank
Is reluctant to swank
Disregardful of those it offends;

Since this poem of mine
Has reached line ninety-nine
It is time that I offered amends.

Dearest Reader, Goodbye!
There's a tear in my eye
For I see that the curtain descends;

Give a roll on the drum
For the moment has come:
I announce that this poem now ends.

*   *   *   *

Lee C.F. Sallows
Nijmegen, June 1982

There was an old glutton of Duns,
Who said, " I'll eat ninety-three buns."
   At the seventy-first,
   He unluckily burst,
So the rest were consumed by his sons.

There was an old person of Ewell,
Whose temper was callous and cruel,
   He projected a book
   At his elderly cook,
For leaving large lumps in his gruel.

To his cook, said a Gaul, in Fashoda,
" Quick, bring me a Scotch and dash
    soda ;
  For I smell a queer smell,
  Which my nose seems to tell,
Is that of last Monday's hash odour ! "

A fastidious fellow of Fife,
Who possessed a Bulgarian wife,
  Said, " Though she's a Bulgar,
  She's really too vulgar,
She *will* eat her peas with a knife ! "

Said a Captain, when cruising off Finland,
" Where can I these cases of gin land ? "
  " Not here," said the pilot,
  " They're such a darned dry lot,
We'll have to convey them all inland."

There was an old fellow of Fladda,
Who said, " I'll walk under that ladder,
  For I deeply despise,
  Superstition's darned lies."
He was bitten next day by an adder !

There was a young fellow of Fleet

There was a young young hoyden of
    Flatholm,
Who foolishly brought a polecat home;
   Said her folks to the wench,
   " What a horrible stench!
How thoughtless of you to bring that
    home!"

There was a young fellow of Fleet,
Who couldn't get boots on his feet;
   For each was as large
   As a moderate-sized barge,
So he wore them quite nude in the street.

There was a young lady of France,
Who kicked up her heels in a dance,
    When they cried, " You're too wild ! "
    She said, as she smiled,
" It's my Gallie *ex* - u - ber - ance ! "

To an aspiarist, living in Friesland,
Said a Scot, " I don't mind if your bees
        land
    On my sporran or kilt,
    But I naturally wilt
When the troublesome pests on my knees
        land ! "

44

A fatuous fellow of Frome,
Played, " God Save the King," on a
    comb ;
    When he played to the people,
    Astride the church steeple,
They took him away to a home.

A pushful young fellow of Girton,
Whenever he put a dress shirt on ;
    By way of a stunt,
    Would let out the front
As space to display an advt. on.

There was a young fellow of Gort,
Who wore on his neck a large wart ;
   Said he, to his uncle,
    " It's a useful carbuncle,
Which serves as a collar support."

There was a young servant of Govan,
Who, in some respects, was a sloven,
   She'd scrub all the floors,
    And polish the doors,
But objected to clean out the oven.

There was a young fellow of Graney,
Incredibly clever and brainy,
   When he put up his gamp,
   If he found it was damp,
He could tell that the weather was rainy !

A leather-lunged lady of Grantham,
Would never take part in the anthem,
   Being told by the prior,
   If her voice reached the choir,
The sound would upset and unman them.

An epicure living at Gratz,
Was exceedingly partial to cats ;
   He relished them toasted,
   Or boiled, baked, or roasted,
Or thoroughly stewed in old hats.

There was a young man of Great Sankey,
Who was so exceedingly lanky,
   He'd stand on a chair,
   When brushing his hair,
And tip-toe to reach for his " hankey."

There was an old person of Greece,
Who ate a large duck and two geese,
 When they said, " Oh what greed ! "
 He replied, " No, indeed !
I've eaten them out of caprice ! "

Said a young lady tourist, from Greenlaw,
" I much resent this quarentine law,
 It's foolish and feudal,
 They've detained my pet poodle,
It's time they repealed such a mean law ! "

There was a small schoolgirl of Guise,
Who wriggled about, ill at ease;
   When her teacher said, " Jane,
   Have you got a pain ? "
She answered, " Oh, no miss, it's fleas ! "

There was an old sportsman of Hatfield,
Who went to hunt rats, in a rat field;
   Said he, " Not one pest
   Has rewarded my quest,
Can they be in this field or that field ? "

A fisherman, fishing at Herm,
Commenced, of a sudden, to squirm;
   When his comrades did cry,
   " Have you swallowed a fly ? "
He gasped, " No, I've swallowed the
     worm ! "

A lively young fellow of Hassocks,
Declared he would look well in cassocks ;
   But, though he enthused,
   The Bishop refused
To ordain him, because of his Jazz socks.

There was a young fellow of Hertford-
    shire,*
Who dallied about with the Ertfordshire ;
  But was no good at any,
  So lost every penny,
And the poor chap is now driving cert-
    fordshire.

There was a young man of Hong Kong,
No girl could endure him for long ;
  It wasn't his actions
  Which caused these refractions
But the fact that his breath was too strong!

*If it be remembered that the contracted form for the name of
this county is pronounced " Harts," the interpretation of
the words which rhyme with it in the above Limerick will
be simple.*

There was a young lady of Hounslow,
Who insisted on wearing her gounslow;
   When chaffed in the street,
   She declared with some heat,
" I cannot help thinking this tounslow ! "

A handsome young fellow of Hove,
Attired in pyjamas of mauve,
   Paraded the Lawns,
   On fine Sabbath morns,
He *was* an original cove !

There was a young blockhead of Hull,
A lorry ran over his skull,
    When they asked, " Are you faint ? "
    He replied, " No, I ain't !
But I'm feeling undoubtedly dull."

A clever young fellow of Huntingdon,*
Could perform some remarkable stunting-
        don,
    He would skate on his nose,
    Brush his hair with his toes,
And pole at one time seven puntingdon.

* *Hunts.*

There was a poor fellow of Hurst,
Who died and was buried—dispersed ;
   Which did him no treason,
   For this was the reason,
He'd grown so obese that he burst !

A funny old person of Hylton,
When he read Robert Burns, put a kilt on ;
   But dressed in a cope
   When reading from Pope,
And a nightshirt when reading from
   Milton.

A curious old person of Hythe,
Amputated his nose with a scythe,
   That he might ascertain
   If he'd writhe with the pain,
Then yelled, " I undoubtedly writhe ! "

There was an old fellow of Inishmore,
Who said, " I feel sure I could finish more
   Of that cold roasted mutton,
   I own I'm a glutton,
And that's why I want to diminish more."

A worldly young lady of Iver,
Once had a fiancé, a diver,
   But broke her engagement,
   To show what her rage meant,
When she found that he hadn't a fiver.

There was a young Jewess of Jackson,
Who bleached her hair till it was flaxen ;
   Said she, " Gents are fond,
   So it's said, of the blonde,
So in future my type will be Saxon."

A motorist, living at Jassy,
Once jilted a lovable lassie;
   Said he, " I know Grace
   Has a beautiful face,
But I'm not very struck with her chassis!"

A greedy old person of Kampot,
Consumed the contents of a jam pot;
   When they said, " You look queer!"
   He answered, " Oh, dear!
I wish I'd not empied that d—— pot!"

A rapacious old rascal of Kars,
Frequented a great many bars ;
    Said he, " You may think
    I am after the drink,
But I'm after the ends of cigars ! "

An ubiquitous lady of Karshi,
Said, " To Persia I'll go and the Shah
      see."
    But she hadn't a card,
    So he said to his guard,
" I will *not* see strange females. Who are
      she ? "

There was a young lady of Keady,
Whose affection for cake was most
     greedy ;
  Though of current or plum
  She would not touch a crumb,
What ho, when she spotted the seedy !

A man in a slop-shop at Kelso,
Said, " I won't buy that coat, for it smells
     so."
  " Tain't the coat thir, ith me,"
  Said old Abrahams, " we
Fumigate all our garments, and well so."

There was a young rip of Kentucky,
Who called a strange lady a ducky ;
   But her husband, a fighter,
   Destroyed the poor blighter.
Some people are always unlucky !

There was a wild spalpeen of Kerry,
Who stood on his head on the ferry ;
   When the mate said, " My son
   You are too full of fun,"
He replied, " No, I'm too full of sherry ! "

There was a young man of Key West,
Who measured ten feet round the chest,
   Said he, " It gives vigour
   And strength to my figure,
But it costs a darned lot for a vest ! "

There was an old gourmand of Kieff,
Who practised this funny belief,
   He always took mustard
   With trifle, or custard,
But never with bacon or beef.

There was a sly flapper of Kilia,
Whose conduct could not have been
    sillier ;
  She walked on flat ground,
  Plainly-skirted and gowned,
But when she climbed hills she was
    frillier.

There was a young wife of Kilrush,
Who went out in pants of red plush ,
  When they asked her, "Why crimson ? "
  She replied, " I've got Jim's on,
Their colour goes well with my blush."

There was an old person of Kohat,
Who made it a rule to wear no hat.
   Said he, " Here it's windier
   Than elsewhere in India,
And the breeze from my noddle would
     blow hat."

Sez Mickey, when visiting Laigle,
To Patrick, " Bedad there's an aigle ! "
   " An aigle ? " sez Pat,
   " Indade it's not that,
Can't you see, ye spalpeen, it's a saygull ! "

A clever young fellow of Lancashire,*
Tried to learn alphabetical Mancashire ;
   When he begged Sir Hall Caine
   The hard words to explain,
His appeal was rejected with thankashire.

There was an old skipper from Largo,
Who n'er was allowed with his cargo,
   To proceed to the shore,
   As he constantly swore,
In a horrible nautical argot.

* *Lancs.*

E

Said the wife of a farmer in Larne,
" My stockings I've torn in that barn,
　　You must buy me some more,
　　To replenish my store."
But the brute merely murmured, " Oh,
　　darn ! "

Said a funny old person of Lask,
" For lodgings such prices they ask,
　　That I will seek lodgin' ease,
　　Like old Diogenes,
By arranging to tenant a cask ! "

There was a young lady of Leek,
Who married a picturesque sheik;
    When he showed her his harem,
    She said, " I can't bear 'em ! "
And returned home to Leek in a pique.

A nervous young man of Lough Foyle,
From the Mistletoe Bough did recoil;
    When they asked, " Are you shy ? "
    He exclaimed, " No, but I
Am frightened of bursting my boil ! "

Said a casual husband of Lugo,
" This evening, I'll to the tattoo go."
   Said his wife, " I would view
   A tattoo, or two, too,
So I'll view the tattoo, too, if you go."

There was a young lady of Lutterworth,
Who queried, " How much is your butter
    worth ? "
   Said the dairyman, " Miss,
   I can recommend this,
It's known far and wide for it's utter
    worth ! "

There was a young lady of Lynton,
Whose face had a very pink tint on ;
    When they asked, " Is it paint ? "
    She replied, " No, it ain't !
I resent such a subject a hint on ! "

Two malapert poets of Lytham,
On an editor called, and took with 'em
    Their Limerick stock,
    Which gave him a shock,
When he found it entirely lacked rhythm.

" Bring a Light! " cried a fool, in Madras

" Bring a light ! " cried a fool, in Madras,
" I will look for that leakage of gas."
   His fun'ral procession
   Made quite an impression,
It took twenty minutes to pass.

A foolish young man of Malaga,
Stabbed himself with a dagger, or da - ger,
   When they asked, " Is your action
   Through a hopeless attraction ? "
He said, " No, it's through drinking much
     Lager."

For a kettle, a minx in Malay,
The shopman objected to pay ;
  But he, for the kettle, meant
  To have a Straits Settlement,
And did so, the very next day.

When Mike, making candles at Mallow,
Fell into a vat of hot tallow ;
  Said his furious pa,
  " This is going too far,
But Michael was always so callow ! "

Said a plain-spoken mother, of Mandalay,
To her daughter, "What makes that
    young Stan delay?
  If you're ready to marry,
  There's no need to tarry,
You're a fool if you let that young—
    Mandelay!"

Observed a young man, of Mauritius,
"To break my engagement's judicious;
  For yesterday, Rose
  Bit the end off my nose,
And I'm rather afraid that she's vicious!"

There was an old fellow of Merstham,
His tailors he ups and he curstham ;
   Said he, " I'm dismayed !
   The bunglers have made
My trousers so tight that I've burstham ! "

There was an old lady of Minster,
Who said, " I will *not* be a spinster ! "
   So proposed to the curate,
   When paying her pew-rate,
Which turned the whole parish aginst
     her.

A flapper who lived in Modena,
Appeared in a music-hall scena,
   Of morals perverse,
   And made matters worse
By her shameless stage name—Miss De
    Meanour !

There is an old Man of the Mumbles,
Who never goes out but he tumbles ;
   The reason, I think,
   Is undoubtedly drink.
No wonder his better half grumbles.

There was an old person of Nairn,
Who lived all his life in a cairn ;
   When they said, " You're a brave man
   To live like a cave man,"
He said, " I've done so since a bairn."

A snail-breeder, living in Nailsworth,
Was asked, " Pray, how much are your
      snails worth ? "
   " If you'll wait," replied he,
   " I will sort them and see,
For a female's worth more than a male's
      worth."

A casual young lady of Nancy,
Was seldom, if ever, romancy ;
   When her beau said, sincerely,
    " I worship you, dearly ! "
She answered, " Good gracious ! Just
    fancy ! "

There was a gay flapper of Nanking,
Who richly deserved a good spanking
   She eloped in a car,
   With a Chinese Hussar,
While the owner his money was banking.

When they asked an old sexton of New-
    bury,
" How many in one day can you bury ? "
  He replied, " If they're thin,
  I can put many in,
And if fat 'uns they be, but a few bury."

A charming young lady of Newent,
On a fast motor-bicycle who went,
  When she sits, now says, " O—er ! "
  For the bicycle threw her,
Because in the mud it askew went.

A cannibal child, of New Guinea,
Said, " I have a pain 'neath my pinny,
  Those mission'ry pies
  I must not gormandize,
If I'd save myself ignominy."

There was a young girl of New Jersey,
Who crept through some undergrowth,
    furzy,
  Said her mother, " How careless,
  Your serge frock would tear less,
I fear you have spoiled your—New
    Jersey ! "

There was a young wife of Newquay,
Who said to her spouse, " I've a flea ! "
　　When he asked, " Will it bite ? "
　　She said, " Turn up the light,
" It's much too dark, darling, to see."

There was an old toper of Newry,
Who drank the contents of a brewery ;
　　His resultant demise
　　Was caused by D.T.'s ;
By unanimous vote of the jury,

A nasty old native of Nijar,
Had a habit which did upon me jar,
 He kept quite a lot
 Of flies in a pot,
And a number of fleas in a flea jar.

With her tears, a young lady of Nish,
Could fill a large plate or a dish ;
 So she went on the screen,
 And in films is now seen,
As the Servian Lillian Gish.

There was a young lady of Norway,
Who emerged—pretty thing—from a
    doorway;
    When a knut said, " What Ho!
    Which way do you go?"
She freezingly answered, "Not your
    way!"

There was an old Croesus of Nottingham-
    shire,*
Of money he simply had pottingham-
    shire;
    He'd his own private train,
    And a large aeroplane,
And many magnificent yottinghamshire.
* *Notts*

There was a pert daughter of Osage,
Who said, " Give me half of your
    sausage."
  Said her mother, " Susannah,
  I don't like your manner,
And the way you endeavour to boss age."

There was a young wifey of Oxted,
Who said, " I've bought seventeen frocks,
    Ted ;
  And to show that my pelf
  Isn't spent all on self,
I've bought you a pair of new socks, Ted."

There was an old woman of Papua,
Who said to her spouse, " What a chap
     you are !
  You seemed to be cursed
  With perennial thirst,
Each night at the brewery tap you are ! "

There was an old girl of Penang,
Who saluted her spouse with a bang ;
  Said she, " In your sleep,
  If you *will* talk, then keep
From using such horrible slang ! "

A trusting young lady of Pennyghent,
Deceived by her beau, a Kilkenny gent,
   Said, " After this warning,
   The male sex I'm scorning,
I vow I will never wed any gent ! "

A beautiful girl of Penzance,
Attended a spirit seance,
   To lighten the tedium,
   She twiced kissed the medium,
Who said, " Do it again, you in*trance !* "

When they asked a great glutton of
    Pinner,
" Do you know where you'll go, you old
    sinner,
    When you die ? " He said, " No,
    But I hope I shall go
To the place where they cook the best
    dinner."

There was a young lady of Pisa,
Whose husband did often displease her ;
    At a poetry recital,
    By a lady of title,
He called out, " You silly old gieser ! "

There was a young fellow of Porthcawl,
Who to Scotland rushed, on a North call ;
   That he might propose
   To a girl in Montrose,
But she didn't say " yes " till his fourth
    call.

A careless young lady of Putney,
Once purchased a bottle of chutney ;
   But the negligent lass
   Fell down with the glass,
And now she is nursing a cut knee.

There was an old person of Ramber,
Who up a cliff started to clamber;
   When they cried, " Oh, you'll fall ! "
   He replied, " Not at all,
I'm merely prospecting for amber."

There was a young maid of Rangoon,
Who eloped with a man in a balloon;
   When a strenuous kiss
   Made them fall out of this,
She said, " We're descending too soon."

A naughty young minx of Ravenna,
When summoned to go to Gehenna,
   Affected great shyness,
   And told His " Black Highness,"
" I won't go without my duenna."

A steadfast young fellow of Reading,
Dressed in blankets attended his wedding;
   Said he, " Ere I rose,
   A thief stole my clothes,
So I've come to be wed in my bedding."

There was a vexed mother of Redruth,
Who spoke from the stair-top and said,
    " Ruth,
  You've been kissing young Ben,
  Since quarter past ten,
It's time you were coming to bed, Ruth !"

A cyclist, awheel in Rhodesia,
Said, " I've never seen a road greasier ; "
  Said the guide, " A mile higher,
  Where it's very much drier,
I'm sure we shall find the—Rhodesia ! "

There was an old man of the Rhone,
Who went to his new telephone,
    When they said, " Number, please ! "
    He gave a loud sneeze,
And said, " I'm just testing the tone."

There was an old toper of Rippingale,
Who wasted his wages in sipping ale ;
    When his wife cried, " You beast ! "
    He said, " Not in the least,
There's every excuse, it is—Rippingale ! "

There was a young pair on the sands,
Who sat in a trance, holding hands,
   And the incoming tide
   Found them thus occupied,
There *was* a young pair on the sands !

A funny old man of St. Ives,
Collected nut-crackers and knives ;
   He'd buy 'em in dozens,
   To give to his cousins,
Or, if they were wed, to their wives.

There was a young female of Sark,
Who was frightened of trees in the dark ;
   When they sneered, " Why such fright ?
   Do you fear they will bite ? "
She said, " No, I'm afeared of their bark!"

Said a Communist looter in Shanghai,
" Unless I resign from this gang, I
   May figure in scenes
   In which British marines
From a gallows may publicly hang I ! "

There was an old man of Shimoga,
Whose face was like that of an ogre ;
   Said the police, " It's unlawful
   To wear features so awful,
You must cover them up in your toga."

There was an old man on the shingle,
Who said, " How I wish I were single ;
   It's nothing but strife,
   Between me and the wife,
Our natures, somehow, do not mingle."

There was a young fellow of Shute,
Who made such a row on a flute,
   He was told by the police
   He must instantly cease,
Or play on a flute that was mute.

There was a young fellow of Sikkim,
Who sought out a rival to lick him ;
   When found, groaning loudly,
   He said, none too proudly,
"He kicked me before I could kick him!"

A lady who lived at South Mimms,
Possessed the most beautiful limbs,
  And the masculine queue
  Ev'ry day longer grew,
When she tripped down the beach for her
    swims.

There was an old woman of Stratton,
With a face like an apple pie, sat on ;
  Said her impolite spouse,
  " Take it out of the house,
It don't look so bad with a hat on ! "

There was a young lady of Stroud,
Whose face would have passed, in a
    crowd ;
  But who had to insert,
  In a crinoline skirt,
Her legs, which were terribly bowed.

There was a young fellow of Sylt,
Who persisted in wearing a kilt ;
  When they said, " You look quaint,
  For a Scotchman you ain't ; "
He said, " No, but my calves are well
    built."

There was a young lady of Sutton

There was a young lady of Sutton,
With the will to become a great glutton
 But, despite ev'ry care,
 She died of despair,
For her mouth was as small as a button!

Said a funny old person of Taft,
" I enjoy a sea-trip on my raft ;
 Than a yacht she costs less,
 Though I'm bound to confess,
When it's windy, there's more of a
  draught ! "

There is an old man of Tangier,
Whose features are certainly queer,
　　For a study discloses
　　Three eyes and four noses,
But only five-eights of an ear.

There was an old man of Tanjore,
Whose nose was a yard long, or more,
　　So he wore the d—— thing
　　In a surgical sling,
To keep it from wiping the floor.

There was a young dancer of Tartary,
Who burst in her leg a small artery ;
   When they asked, " This mischance,
   Was it caused through a dance ? "
She said, " No, through being too tight
     gartery."

Said an angry old person of Tewin,
To his wife, " You will bring me to
     rui— in ;
   It's highly improper
   To take my best topper,
And use it for mixing the glue in ! "

There was an old man of Thibet,
The quaintest of all I have met;
 Said he, " I find onions
  Are good for my bunions,
And so I eat all I can get."

There was a young fellow of Thurles,
Who loved, at one time, nineteen girls;
 His conduct was reckless,
  He gave each a necklace,
Composed of real rubies and pearls.

When they asked an old fellow of Thurso,
" Why *do* you persistently curse so ? "
   Said he, " It's my wife,
   She's the plague of my life,
Her tongue every day *will* converse so ! "

There was an old girl of the Tiber,
Whom I fear was a hardened imbiber ;
   For she walked on the pier,
   In a costume most queer,
Made solely of cocoa-nut fibre.

There is a young lady of Tilsit,
When she sees a flea she ne'r kills it.
    Said she, " It does right,
    My person to bite,
I can't interfere—Heaven wills it ! "

A flapper at school at Tirnova,
Once stood on her head 'midst the clover ;
    Said the mistress, " Such pranks
    Must be punished with spanks,
Just go to my desk and—Tirnova ! "

Said a Communist looter in Tow Law,
" Your goods are all mine, I know no
    law ! "
  But the shopkeeper's boot
  Soon instructed the brute
In a primitive law, known as—Toe Law !

In the backyard, a bold minx of Towton,
Danced the Charleston with nary a clout
    on ;
  Till her shocked mother spoke,
  " You must put on your toque,
I object to you dancing with nowt on."

A violent old girl of Tobago,
Was known as a vicious virago;
  When they said to her, " Why ? "
  She screamed in reply,
" It's through this 'ere plaguey lumbago!"

There was a young lady of Trim,
Who attempted the Channel to swim;
  But a ravenous porpoise,
  Intercepted her corpus,
We will now sing the fifty-fifth hymn.

There was a small daughter of Trinidad,
Who said, " Oh I do feel a ninny, Dad ;
  Your jar of red ink,
  I've spilled, and I think,
It's all upset down my new pinny, Dad."

There was a young damsel of Troy,
Whose manners were cautious and coy :
  When she went for a sail,
  And there came a slight gale,
She immediately clung to a boy !

Said a pedagogue, kindly, of Troyes,
" It is true, sir, that boys will be boys ;
    But when in my bed
    I find stale buttered bread,
I cannot help losing my poise ! "

There was a young husband of Troyes,
Who was told by the nurse, " It's three
      boys ! "
    Said he, " Deary me !
    I certainly see
Excessive paternity cloys ! "

There was an old girl of Uganda,
Renowned for her coolness and candour,
   When, during abuse,
    Her spouse yelled, " You goose ! "
She quickly retorted, " Uganda ! "

There was a young lady of Usk,
Who had one large tooth, like a tusk ;
   A dentiform growth
    Which rendered her loath
To walk in the streets before dusk.

Said a tourist, shown round Utopia,
" It's funny there's not any soap 'ere."
   Said the Mayor, " Not at all,
   There ain't any call,
For dirt never has any scope 'ere ! "

There was an old man of Vementry,
Who made an unauthorised entry,
   Into Buckingham Palace,
   And though it seems callous,
Was fatally shot by the sentry.

Said the Mayor of a town, near Vesuvius,
" We shall welcome old Jupiter Pluvius,
   To come with his rains,
   And cleanse the town drains,
From these troublesome, horrid effluvias!"

Said a wife, to her hubby, in Vigo,
" To that scandalous cabaret, why go ?
   Where saucy young minxes,
   Indulge in high jinkses,
The next time you go there, then I go ! "

Said a breeder of goldfish, at Wandsworth,
" How much are the fish in my ponds
worth ? "
    Said an expert, " For fee,
    I will sort them and see,
For a brunette's worth less than a
blonde's worth."

There was a young lady of Wantage,
Whose nose was her great disadvantage,
    For the rubicund tip
    Adjoined her top lip,
Which quite spoilt her facial frontage.

A frenzied old fellow of Ware,
Once stood on his head during prayer
    Sobbed he, " I'm converted ! "
    Said they, " No, inverted ;
Henceforth you must worship elsewhere ! "

There was a bad actor of Watton,
Shakespearean plays he was hot on ;
    When billed to play, " Hamlet,"
    The people said, " Damn let
Us go to the pictures, he's rotten ! "

An artful young artist, of Wesel,
Delighted young ladies to squeeze all;
   So asked them on Sundays,
   And Thursdays and Mondays,
To come round and look at his easel.

Said a musical chap of the Wetterhorn,
" I would play on a horn—so I'll getter-
     horn."
   But the horn was so flat,
   That the folks cried, " Stop that !
If you must play a horn, get a better
     horn ! "

There was a young lady of Woking,
Who suddenly took up pipe smoking;
    And smoked such strong shag,
    From a small canvas bag,
That she set all those near her a-choking.

There is an old city, called Worms,
When a gourmet comes near it he squirms;
    And in it won't feed,
    No wonder, indeed,
For it's famed for it's " Diet of Worms ! "

There was an old toper of Yale,
Who used to drink beer from a pail ;
    If he couldn't get that,
    He would use a top hat,
His thirst was so very wholesale.

There was an old fellow of Yate,
Who swallowed, " One over the eight."
    And was burnt to a cinder,
    When striking a tinder,
To kindle a fire in the grate.

There was a young bounder of Yorkshire,*
Who fractured his hostesses' forkshire;
    By making a campaign,
    When they brought in the champagne,
In respect of extracting the corkshire.

A Zo-ologist's daughter, of Zug,
Said " Pa, what is that on the rug ? "
    Cried he, " Goodness gracious !
    How very vexatious,
I fear it's a blood-sucking insect of the
        Cimex lectularius species ! "

* *Yorks*

LIST OF LIMERICKS

(Arranged according to the " Key " word in each)

C—*continued*

Chertsey
Clifton
Colon
Cromer
Crook
Cupar
Cutch

D

Dakota
Darton
Darvel
Dawlish
Deal
Detmold
Dijon
Duns

E

Ewell

F

Fashoda
Fife
Finland
Fladda
Flatholm
Fleet
France
Friesland
Frome

G

Girton
Gort
Govan
Graney
Grantham
Gratz
Great Sankey
Greece
Greenlaw
Guise

H	K
Hatfield	Kampot
Herm	Kars
Hassocks	Karshi
Hertfordshire	Keady
Hong Kong	Kelso
Hounslow	Kentucky
Hove	Kerry
Hull	Key West
Huntingdon	Kieff
Hurst	Kilia
Hylton	Kilrush
Hythe	Kohat

I	L
Inishmore	Laigle
Iver	Lancashire
	Largo
J	Larne
	Lask
Jackson	Leek
Jassy	Lough Foyle

L—*continued*

Lugo
Lutterworth
Lynton
Lytham

M

Madras
Malaga
Malay
Mallow
Mandalay
Mauritius
Merstham
Minster
Modena
Mumbles

N

Nairn
Nailsworth

N—*continued*

Nancy
Nanking
Newbury
Newent
New Guinea
New Jersey
Newquay
Newry
Nijar
Nish
Norway
Nottinghamshire

O

Osage
Oxted

P

Papua
Penang

P—continued

Pennyghent
Penzance
Pinner
Pisa
Porthcawl
Putney

R

Ramber
Rangoon
Ravenna
Reading
Redruth
Rhodesia
Rhone
Rippingale

S

Sands
St. Ives

S—continued

Sark
Shanghai
Shimoga
Shingle
Shute
Sikkim
South Mimms
Stratton
Stroud
Sylt
Sutton

T

Taft
Tangier
Tanjore
Tartary
Tewin
Thibet
Thurles
Thurso